HANDBOOK
Butterflies & Moths

Written by

Camilla de la Bedoyere

Miles Kelly

First published in 2012 by Miles Kelly Publishing Ltd
Harding's Barn, Bardfield End Green, Thaxted, Essex, CM6 3PX, UK

This edition printed in 2013

2 4 6 8 10 9 7 5 3 1

Publishing Director *Belinda Gallagher*
Creative Director *Jo Cowan*
Editor *Sarah Parkin*
Cover Designer *Jo Cowan*
Designers *Simon Lee, Kayleigh Allen*
Image Manager *Liberty Newton*
Production Manager *Elizabeth Collins*
Reprographics *Stephan Davis, Thom Allaway*
The Wildlife Trusts Advisors *Nick Acheson, Adam Cormack, Amy Lewis*

Miles Kelly would like to thank **The Wildlife Trusts** for their valuable contribution to this book.

ISBN 978-1-78209-169-1

Printed in China

British Library Cataloguing-in-Publication Data
A catalogue record for this book is available from the British Library

ACKNOWLEDGEMENTS

All artworks are from the Miles Kelly Artwork Bank

The publishers would like to thank the following sources for the use of their photographs:
Key: t = top, b = bottom, c = centre, l = left, r = right, bg = background

Ardea 40 John Mason (JLMO)
FLPA 9(t) Peter Entwistle, (c) Ian Rose, (b) David T. Grewcock; 32 Derek Middleton; 66 Martin B Withers; 72 Nigel Cattlin; 74 G E Hyde; 78 Joke Stuurman-Huitema; 84 Nigel Cattlin
Fotolia.com 2–3(bg) Günther Schad; 5(c) StudioAraminta; 8(tl) MLA photography; 12–13(bg); 18; 52 Christina Bernhardsen; 82 Gucio_55
iStockphoto.com 6 Blue Plinney, Nymph jeromewhittingham
NHPA 68 David Chapman; 90 Robert Thompson
Shutterstock.com front cover Radka Palenikova; 5(t) Jens Stolt; 6 Skipper Marco Uliana, Swallowtail Alslutsky, White Steve McWilliam, Hairstreak MarkMirror, Copper Emjay Smith; 8(tr) AdamEdwards, (bl) Martina I. Meyer, (br) David Benton; 12 R.S.Jegg; 13(bg) Jakub Krechowicz; 14 MarkMirror; 16 Christian Musat; 20 Steve Byland; 22 Ziga Camernik; 24 Alslutsky; 26 P.Schwartz; 28 Mircea Bezergheanu; 30 MarkMirror; 34 Birute Vijeikiene; 36 Florian Andronache; 38 JonBrackpool-Photography; 42 A.S.Floro; 44; 46 Shutterschock; 48 Fotoveto; 50 Kirsanov; 54 imortalcris; 56 Torsten Dietrich; 58 Igor Semenov; 60 Steve McWilliam; 62 Rasmus Holmboe Dahl; 64 Alslutsky; 70 Christian Musat; 76 HartmutMorgenthal; 80 Slawomir Kruz; 86 Henrik Larsson; 88 Chekaramit; 92 Marek R. Swadzba; 94 Martin Fowler
The Wildlife Trusts 96 Amy Lewis

Every effort has been made to acknowledge the source and copyright holder of each picture.
Miles Kelly Publishing apologises for any unintentional errors or omissions.

www.mileskelly.net   info@mileskelly.net

www.factsforprojects.com

Contents

Checklist: Mark off your butterfly and moth sightings in the tick boxes above.

I remember watching gobsmacked as I witnessed the everyday miracle of a chrysalis rupture to reveal the most bizarre-looking crumpled mess! Which, given twenty minutes to compose itself and pump blood into its veins, took the perfect form of an adult butterfly.

From that moment I was hooked on these insects and their mainly nocturnal counterparts, the moths. It wasn't just a love affair with the obvious beauty of their wings, but also with the beauty of their lives, from their complicated life-cycles, to the tricks they employ to baffle predators, and of course their ability to tell us so much about the health of the world we live in.

Inside, there are over 40 butterfly and moth species to spot, and each is accurately presented. There's also space for your own sketches, photos and notes. Instructions on how to encourage butterflies and moths into your garden will help you create a haven for these fascinating creatures.

This book is the perfect companion for a young naturalist about to embark on a journey of endless wonder and fascination. It not only helps to put a 'name to the face' (an essential first step to understanding), but also to springboard them into the detailed depths of the amazing lives of butterflies and moths.

Nick Baker

Become a butterfly and moth detective

All nature detectives need to be prepared, and that is especially true for a lepidopterist (someone who studies butterflies and moths). These fragile flying insects don't always settle for long, so you need to be ready.

SPOTTING BUTTERFLIES AND MOTHS

1 Most adult butterflies and day-flying moths feed on nectar from flowering plants. Gardens, parks, meadows, woods, wastelands, coastal areas and hedgerows are all good places to spot them.

2 When you see a butterfly or moth you need to get as close as you can before it flies away. Move slowly and quietly, and look for key features such as colours, patterns, spots and wing shape.

Checklist

O colouring pens and pencils
O camera
O sun hat and cream on hot days
O warm clothing on cool days
O magnifying glass
O bottle of water

Equipment

Fill in the pages of this book with your notes and sketches. Using a camera to photograph what you see will help you to identify it accurately.

Warnings

Butterflies and moths cannot harm you, but some caterpillars can. Caterpillars with bright colours or hairy backs might irritate your skin.

Look out for stinging plants and insects.

If a butterfly or moth lands on you, stay still and enjoy watching its behaviour. Do not be tempted to touch its wings – they are delicate and easily damaged.

The Lepidopterist's Code

1 You must have an adult's permission to go exploring, and they must know where you will be at all times.

2 Respect nature and habitats: do not catch butterflies and moths, or remove caterpillars from their food plants.

3 Always take your litter home with you.

What are the differences?

Butterflies and moths belong to a single group of insects called Lepidopterans. There are some simple ways to tell them apart, but as with all rules there are exceptions!

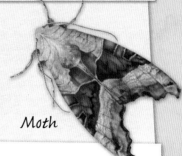

Moth

Butterfly

How to tell them apart

1 Butterflies are most active in the day, but most moths are more active at night.

2 Butterfly bodies are usually slender and smooth, but many moth bodies are thick and furry.

3 Moths are more likely to have dull colours, while butterflies are often brightly coloured and patterned.

4 Butterfly antennae often have club-ends, but moth antennae are usually thin or feathery.

Identifying butterflies

Scientists put animals and plants into smaller groups by using key features, such as size, colour and shape. Use this guide to help you identify the butterflies you find.

Skipper

Skippers, Swallowtails and Whites	Hairstreaks, Coppers and Blues	Nymphs
Skippers Small with heavy bodies and big eyes. Antennae tips are often bent backwards. **Swallowtails** Large with striking patterns. Hind wings are often long, with 'tails'. **Whites** Usually pale coloured, with dark spots.	Small but often brightly coloured butterflies. They may have a metallic sheen on their wings.	Medium to large in size and mostly bright-coloured. The first pair of legs is small and the butterflies may look as if they only have four legs, not six.

Swallowtail

Hairstreak

Copper

Nymph

White

Blue

6

Special life-cycle

Butterflies and moths have an extraordinary life-cycle. As they grow from eggs into adults they go through a larval stage. A larva, or caterpillar, looks very different from an adult. Changing from a caterpillar into a moth or butterfly is an example of an incredible process called metamorphosis.

Larva

Egg

1

- Eggs are often laid on the underside of a food plant's leaves.
- They are often white or pale green, so they are camouflaged on a leaf.
  - Eggs may be oval or round.
  - They may be laid singly or in clusters.

2

- Newly-hatched caterpillars are small, but they quickly grow.
- As a caterpillar grows it sheds, or moults, its old skin.
- Caterpillars feed on the food plant and they must eat, eat and eat – to gain weight.
- Some caterpillars' patterns and colours warn predators to stay away.

4

Adult

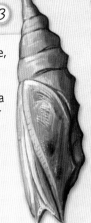

Pupa   **3**

- After growing to full size, the caterpillar pupates (becomes a pupa).
- A pupa is also know as a chrysalis (butterflies) or a cocoon (moths).
- Inside the pupa, the insect's adult body develops.
- Some butterflies spend the winter in this state.

- The adult butterfly or moth emerges from the pupa. Its soft wings must dry before it can fly.
- Most adults feed on sugary nectar produced by flowers. Some adult moths don't feed at all.
- Males and females mate, and the females lay eggs.
- An adult butterfly is known as an imago.

Creating a butterfly garden

Encouraging butterflies to visit your garden is a great way to develop your skills as a nature detective. These insects will also encourage more plants to grow, by helping seeds to develop. While they feed, butterflies transfer pollen from one flower to another. This pollen will fertilize the flowers' eggs, which can then turn into seeds.

Buddleia is the 'butterfly bush'

Caterpillars and butterflies can be fussy feeders. Some caterpillars only eat leaves of particular plants, such as stinging nettles, and some butterflies are attracted to particular flowers, where they feast on the sweet nectar the flowers make.

Lavender has a strong perfume

Grow herbs, such as oregano

Tips to attract butterflies

- Grow flowers in sunny spots. Butterflies need to warm up in the sunshine before they can fly, feed and mate.
- Choose a range of plants, so there are flowers growing from spring all the way through to autumn.

Michaelmas daisies flower in autumn

- Select flowers that have bright colours and strong scents. You will find other pollinating insects, such as bees, come to visit too.

Creating a moth garden

Pale-coloured, nectar-rich and sweet-scented flowers will attract moths that are active in the day and at night. Some flowers produce their scent in the evening and are popular with night-flying insects.

Look out for the colourful six-spot burnet

Tips to attract moths

- Let an area of your garden go wild. Let any wild grasses grow tall and, in a nearby space, plant some wildflowers.
- Encourage stinging nettles to grow. You can keep them in a large container that is dug into the ground to stop them spreading everywhere!
- Avoid using chemicals, such as weed-killers and pesticides, anywhere in the garden. They will kill all insects.

Elephant hawk-moths feed on honeysuckle nectar

Spotting moths

Most moths come out at night, making it difficult to find them. Moth detectives can overcome this problem by setting up a moth trap.

1 Spread a white sheet by a fence or wall, making sure some of it is resting on the ground.
2 Shine a very bright torch on the sheet and wait for the moths to come.
3 When you have finished your investigations, turn the light off and leave the sheet for a while, so the moths can safely move away when they are ready.

Scientists use light to attract moths

How to use this book

*B*utterfly and moth detectives like to keep records of what they have seen, and you can do that by filling in the pages of this book. There are spaces for your notes, sketches and photographs.

Seen it?
Tick this area if you spot the photofile subject. These show something different to the main illustration.

Photofile
Photo of the species in its natural habitat, plus extra information. Some show the caterpillar.

My observations
Make notes about your sightings and surroundings here. For example, write down where you were, the date and time of day, and also the weather. Then you can make a note of what you have found and what it was doing.

My drawings and photos
Fill these spaces with your sketches and photographs.

Photos: Concentrate on taking photos of the whole insect and its habitat. You will need plenty of sunlight, but avoid very bright sunshine because it causes strong black shadows. Make sure your shadow is not cast over your find.

Drawings: Use a soft pencil, such as 2B, because the lead is easy to rub out. You don't need to draw the whole butterfly or moth. For example, you could just draw the wings from above or below.

MY OBSERVATIONS

Location:

Time/date:

The weather is:

What have I found?

What was it doing?

SEEN IT?

Females' wings have orange borders and white edges. They look similar to both brown argus and female chalkhill blue butterflies.

♀

MY DRAWINGS AND PHOTOS

I saw this butterfly in: March ○   April ○   May ○   Ju

24

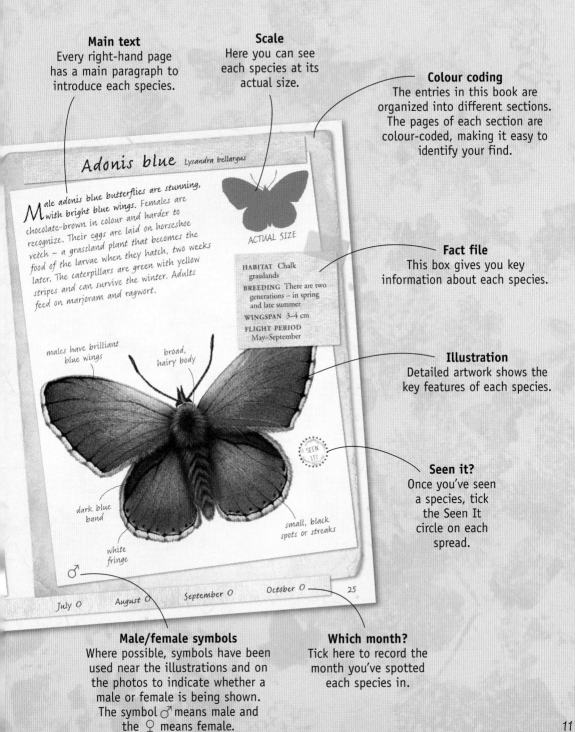

Main text
Every right-hand page has a main paragraph to introduce each species.

Scale
Here you can see each species at its actual size.

Colour coding
The entries in this book are organized into different sections. The pages of each section are colour-coded, making it easy to identify your find.

Adonis blue *Lysandra bellargus*

Male adonis blue butterflies are stunning, with bright blue wings. Females are chocolate-brown in colour and harder to recognize. Their eggs are laid on horseshoe vetch – a grassland plant that becomes the food of the larvae when they hatch, two weeks later. The caterpillars are green with yellow stripes and can survive the winter. Adults feed on marjoram and ragwort.

ACTUAL SIZE

HABITAT Chalk grasslands

BREEDING There are two generations – in spring and late summer

WINGSPAN 3–4 cm

FLIGHT PERIOD May–September

Fact file
This box gives you key information about each species.

Illustration
Detailed artwork shows the key features of each species.

males have brilliant blue wings

broad, hairy body

SEEN IT?

Seen it?
Once you've seen a species, tick the Seen It circle on each spread.

dark blue band

small, black spots or streaks

white fringe

♂

July ○   August ○   September ○   October ○   25

Male/female symbols
Where possible, symbols have been used near the illustrations and on the photos to indicate whether a male or female is being shown. The symbol ♂ means male and the ♀ means female.

Which month?
Tick here to record the month you've spotted each species in.

MY OBSERVATIONS

Location:

Time/date:

The weather is:

What have I found?

What was it doing?

Brimstones usually feed with their wings closed and upright. They particularly like purple flowers, such as thistles.

MY DRAWINGS AND PHOTOS

I saw this butterfly in: March O   April O   May O   June O

Brimstone *Gonepteryx rhamni*

These butterflies are widespread around Britain and other parts of Europe and North Africa. The bluish-green larvae feed on buckthorn leaves and the adults live on a diet of nectar from flowers, such as buddleia. The adults emerge from their chrysalises in July and live until the following summer, after a winter hibernation.

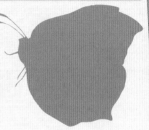

ACTUAL SIZE

HABITAT Woodland and scrub

BREEDING Eggs are laid in May, larvae pupate in June/July and adults emerge two weeks later

WINGSPAN Up to 6 cm

FLIGHT PERIOD March–September

males are bright yellow in colour (females are greenish-white)

orange spot on each wing

undersides of wings are greenish

SEEN IT?

♂

MY OBSERVATIONS

Location: _____

Time/date: _____

The weather is: _____

_____

What have I found?

_____

What was it doing?

_____

_____

_____

The female has two spots on each forewing. Males normally have a single faint spot on each forewing.

♀

MY DRAWINGS AND PHOTOS

I saw this butterfly in: March ○   April ○   May ○   June ○

Green-veined white *Pieris napi*

Although these butterflies are widespread, they are not often seen in gardens. Green-veined whites feed on wild plants that are found in hedgerows, open grasslands and along riverbanks. The sexes look similar except for their black spots. Males often gather around mud, where they can find nutrients to eat. This is known as 'mud-puddling'. Green larvae hatch from little white eggs and feed on leaves.

ACTUAL SIZE

HABITAT Damp places and grasslands

BREEDING Eggs are laid singly and hatch in about a week. Up to three generations may be laid in a summer

WINGSPAN 4–5 cm

FLIGHT PERIOD May–September

wings are mostly white with some spots

long antennae

hind wings have bold green streaks

SEEN IT?

MY OBSERVATIONS

Location: _____

Time/date: _____

The weather is: _____

_____

What have I found? _____

_____

What was it doing? _____

_____

_____

_____

Male skippers spend much of their time perching inside their territories, especially in mornings and evenings.

♂

MY DRAWINGS AND PHOTOS

I saw this butterfly in: March ○ April ○ May ○ June ○

Large skipper *Ochlodes faunus*

*B*etween June and August, large skippers fly around flowering plants in search of nectar to feed on. Adults particularly like brambles and thistles. Male large skippers are territorial, and will chase away other males that stray into their area. It is difficult to find the green larvae, which hide within 'tents' made of folded blades of grass. These butterflies are widespread in England and Wales.

ACTUAL SIZE

HABITAT Sheltered grasslands, parks and hedgerows

BREEDING Females normally lay their white eggs during the early afternoon

WINGSPAN 3–3.5 cm

FLIGHT PERIOD June–August

males have a thick, dark band in the centre of the forewing

large eyes

SEEN IT?

deep orange-brown colour

patches of pale orange or gold on forewings

♂

MY OBSERVATIONS

Location: _____

Time/date: _____

The weather is: _____

_____

What have I found? _____

_____

What was it doing? _____

_____

_____

_____

As the caterpillars feed, they store toxins (poisons) from the food plant in their bodies. Their hairy, spotted skin warns birds that they taste bad.

SEEN IT?

MY DRAWINGS AND PHOTOS

I saw this butterfly in: March O   April O   May O   June O

Large white *Pieris brassicae*

Large white butterflies are often seen fluttering around cabbage and Brussels sprout plants. These garden crops are favourite foods of the yellow-and-black larvae, and the undersides of the leaves often hide patches of yellow eggs. When the larvae hatch, they can eat through entire leaves. Larvae that hatch late in the season form pupae to survive the winter, emerging as adults in April.

ACTUAL SIZE

HABITAT Gardens, farms, fields and parks

BREEDING There are two or three generations a year and females can lay hundreds of eggs at a time

WINGSPAN 6 cm

FLIGHT PERIOD April–September

females have two spots on forewings, males have none

undersides of wings are greyish-white

underside of the body is pale

SEEN IT?

♀

MY OBSERVATIONS

Location: _____

Time/date: _____

The weather is: _____
_____

What have I found? _____
_____

What was it doing? _____
_____
_____
_____

This is a male small white, with one black spot on each forewing. Females have two spots on each forewing.

♂

MY DRAWINGS AND PHOTOS

I saw this butterfly in: March O   April O   May O   June O

Small white *Pieris rapae*

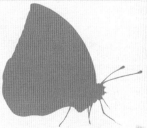

Like its cousin, the large white, this butterfly is commonly known as a cabbage white. Adults suck nectar from flowers such as dandelions, and larvae eat the leaves of cabbages, or similar plants. Adults can often be seen flying upwards in spirals, performing mating rituals. They breed in the summer and the second generation spends winter as chrysalises.

ACTUAL SIZE

HABITAT Gardens and fields

BREEDING The larva is green, with a yellowish line down its back

WINGSPAN 4.5 cm

FLIGHT PERIOD April–October

females have two black spots on each forewing

soft body covered with bristles

long, tube-like mouthparts

white, cream or pale yellow in colour

SEEN IT?

♀

MY OBSERVATIONS

Location: _____

Time/date: _____

The weather is: _____

_____

What have I found? _____

_____

What was it doing? _____

_____

_____

_____

As it grows big and plump, the larva turns green, with black-and-orange markings. It gives off a foul smell to ward off predators.

SEEN IT?

MY DRAWINGS AND PHOTOS

I saw this butterfly in: March ○   April ○   May ○   June ○

Swallowtail *Papilio machaon*

Britain's largest butterflies are attractive insects. Their name describes the long 'tails' that grow at the back of their hind wings. Unusually, their underwings are also bright and colourful. Larvae feed on milk parsley and, when young, resemble bird droppings, which fools possible predators.

ACTUAL SIZE

HABITAT Marshland

BREEDING Eggs are laid in early summer and hatch immediately. The larvae pupate in autumn

WINGSPAN Up to 8 cm

FLIGHT PERIOD May–August

yellow wings with black veins

long, black 'tails'

hind wings have a band of blue and a red spot

SEEN IT?

July ○   August ○   September ○   October ○

23

MY OBSERVATIONS

Location:

Time/date:

The weather is:

What have I found?

What was it doing?

MY DRAWINGS AND PHOTOS

Females' wings have orange borders and white edges. They look similar to both brown argus and female chalkhill blue butterflies.

SEEN IT?

♀

I saw this butterfly in: March O   April O   May O   June O

Adonis blue *Lysandra bellargus*

Male adonis blue butterflies are stunning, with bright blue wings. Females are chocolate-brown in colour and harder to recognize. Their eggs are laid on horseshoe vetch – a grassland plant that becomes the food of the larvae when they hatch, two weeks later. The caterpillars are green with yellow stripes and can survive the winter. Adults feed on marjoram and ragwort.

ACTUAL SIZE

HABITAT Chalk grasslands

BREEDING There are two generations – in spring and late summer

WINGSPAN 3–4 cm

FLIGHT PERIOD May–September

males have brilliant blue wings

broad, hairy body

dark blue band

white fringe

small, black spots or streaks

SEEN IT?

♂

MY OBSERVATIONS

Location: _____

Time/date: _____

The weather is: _____

_____

What have I found? _____

_____

What was it doing? _____

_____

_____

_____

Both males and females are brown, but their underwings are spectacular, with white, black and orange markings.

MY DRAWINGS AND PHOTOS

I saw this butterfly in: March ○   April ○   May ○   June ○

Brown argus *Aricia agestis*

Some butterflies can fly considerable distances, but these butterflies rarely travel more than a few hundred metres. They prefer regions in southern Britain with chalky grasslands and favour warm, sheltered places. Adults may be seen fluttering around their food plants – marjoram, thyme, white clover and ragwort.

ACTUAL SIZE

HABITAT Short, open grasslands

BREEDING Eggs are laid one at a time, and hatch after about one week

WINGSPAN 2.5–3 cm

FLIGHT PERIOD June–August

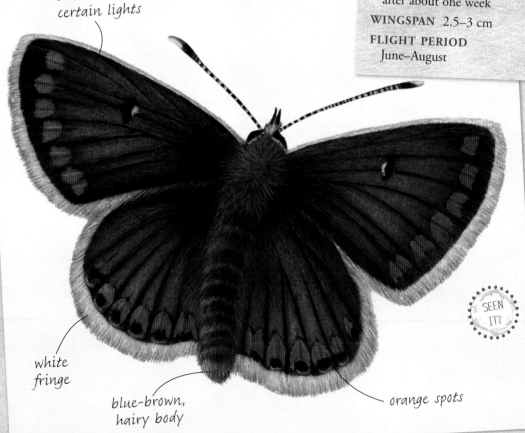

blue sheen in certain lights

white fringe

blue-brown, hairy body

orange spots

SEEN IT?

July ○   August ○   September ○   October ○

27

MY OBSERVATIONS

Location: _____

Time/date: _____

The weather is: _____

_____

What have I found? _____

_____

What was it doing? _____

_____

_____

_____

Males are easier to spot than females, with their brighter colour and more active lifestyle. They fly around, searching for females.

♂

MY DRAWINGS AND PHOTOS

I saw this butterfly in: March ○   April ○   May ○   June ○

Common blue *Polyommatus icarus*

These pretty butterflies may be seen between May and October, when they feed on nectar. They are most common around large, flat-headed flowers, especially in meadows or near roadsides. The larvae are green with yellow stripes along their sides and a dark line down their backs. They feed on the leaves of plants such as white clover and bird's-foot trefoil.

ACTUAL SIZE

HABITAT Grasslands, dunes and wastelands

BREEDING Two to three summer generations in warmer regions, but only one generation in cooler places

WINGSPAN 3–4 cm

FLIGHT PERIOD May–October

males have violet-blue upperwings and females have brown

thin, black border

long antennae

undersides of wings are grey or beige

orange markings and black spots on the undersides

males have blue colouring near the body

SEEN IT?

♂

July ○   August ○   September ○   October ○

MY OBSERVATIONS

Location: _____

Time/date: _____

The weather is: _____

_____

What have I found? _____

_____

What was it doing? _____

_____

_____

_____

This butterfly always rests with its wings closed. It gets its name from the streak of pale spots.

MY DRAWINGS AND PHOTOS

I saw this butterfly in: March ○   April ○   May ○   June ○

Green hairstreak *Callophrys rubi*

M ales and females look similar, but can be told apart by their behaviour. Males usually stay in their territories, waiting for females to pass by. Females are very active, fluttering between flowers looking for food, or searching for places to lay their eggs. The larvae are short and stubby. They feed on leaves and buds, but as they age they may feed on each other.

ACTUAL SIZE

HABITAT Hedgerows, moors, hillsides, wasteland and heaths

BREEDING Eggs are laid one at a time and hatch after one or two weeks

WINGSPAN 2.5–3.5 cm

FLIGHT PERIOD April–July

tops of the wings are brown, but they are only seen in flight

green underwings provide camouflage

faint line of white spots

SEEN IT?

MY OBSERVATIONS

Location: _____

Time/date: _____

The weather is: _____

_____

What have I found? _____

_____

What was it doing? _____

_____

_____

_____

This female, with its pale purple streaks, basks on an oak leaf and warms its body ready for flight.

SEEN IT?

♀

MY DRAWINGS AND PHOTOS

I saw this butterfly in: March ○   April ○   May ○   June ○

Purple hairstreak _Neozephyrus quercus_

Purple hairstreaks live in oak woodlands, and their larvae feed on oak buds. They are found in England, Wales and some parts of Scotland, thriving in warm conditions. These butterflies flutter in groups around treetops, searching for food, mates or places to lay their eggs. Males have a purple sheen to their wings, and females have purple marks on their forewings. The pupae survive the winter in the topsoil or leaf litter.

ACTUAL SIZE

HABITAT Oak woodlands

BREEDING Eggs are laid in late summer, and larvae hatch the following spring

WINGSPAN 3–4 cm

FLIGHT PERIOD July–September

males have dark and white borders on the forewings

both males and females have purple on their wings

creamy-white line on underside

orange markings on underside

underside is grey-brown

SEEN IT?

♂

MY OBSERVATIONS

Location:

Time/date:

The weather is:

What have I found?

What was it doing?

The colours of small coppers can vary greatly, although their underwings are usually orange and brown with spots.

MY DRAWINGS AND PHOTOS

I saw this butterfly in: March ○   April ○   May ○   June ○

Small copper Lycaena phlaeas

These bright, colourful insects are seen throughout Britain, in many habitats. Males are often seen resting in the sunshine, on the ground or on a warm stone. They wait for passing females and fly upwards to attack any other insects that pass overhead. Eggs are usually laid on sorrel leaves, which the larvae will feast on. The short, plump larvae moult four or five times before pupating.

ACTUAL SIZE

HABITAT Grasslands, moors, coastal areas, fields and gardens

BREEDING There may be up to four generations in a single year

WINGSPAN 2.5–3.5 cm

FLIGHT PERIOD April–October

brown band near edge of wing

orange-copper colour with black spots

all four wings have a pale fringe

SEEN IT?

pointed 'tails'

MY OBSERVATIONS

Location: _____

Time/date: _____

The weather is: _____

_____

What have I found? _____

_____

What was it doing? _____

_____

_____

_____

The larvae are black, with red-and-white markings, and red spines. They look like bird droppings to predators.

MY DRAWINGS AND PHOTOS

I saw this butterfly in: March O April O May O June O

Comma *Polygonia c-album*

 With dull patterns on the underside of their wings, commas can be difficult to see among dead leaves. This camouflage helps to protect them from predators when they overwinter in log piles or holes in trees. Commas live in woodlands where they can find flowers to supply them with leaves as larvae and nectar as adults.

ACTUAL SIZE

long, slender antennae

long, sucking mouthparts

furry body

orange-brown wings with dark markings

ragged edges to wings

SEEN IT?

HABITAT Woods and gardens

BREEDING Females can lay up to 275 eggs at a time and there may be two generations in one summer

WINGSPAN 4–5.5 cm

FLIGHT PERIOD March–October

July ⭘　　　August ⭘　　　September ⭘　　　October ⭘

MY OBSERVATIONS

Location:

Time/date:

The weather is:

What have I found?

What was it doing?

Many fritillaries have this characteristic chequered appearance, with orange-and-black markings.

MY DRAWINGS AND PHOTOS

I saw this butterfly in: March O   April O   May O   June O

Dark green fritillary
Argynnis aglaja

These butterflies are mostly orange and black, but they get their name from the dark green tinge on the undersides of their wings. They are found throughout Britain. Adults emerge from their pupae in June, and they are strong fliers that dart from flower to flower, sucking nectar. After the larvae hatch in late summer, they rest until spring and only then start feeding.

ACTUAL SIZE

HABITAT Open grasslands and coastal areas

BREEDING Each female can lay hundreds of yellow eggs

WINGSPAN Up to 7 cm

FLIGHT PERIOD June–September

black spots cover the wings

large, hairy body

males have larger bodies than females

undersides have a hint of green

♂

SEEN IT?

MY OBSERVATIONS

Location: _____

Time/date: _____

The weather is: _____

_____

What have I found? _____

_____

What was it doing? _____

_____

_____

_____

The appearance of the large heath caterpillar mimics the long, green, slender blades of grass, its food plant.

MY DRAWINGS AND PHOTOS

I saw this butterfly in: March O April O May O June O

Large heath *Coenonympha tullia*

It is difficult to spot large heath butterflies because they prefer damp habitats where it is hard to walk. In northern Scotland they tend to have fewer spots on their wings than those that live elsewhere. The larvae feed on a range of wild plants, including cottongrasses and rushes. The adults suck nectar from flowers such as heather.

ACTUAL SIZE

HABITAT Bogs and damp moorlands

BREEDING Eggs are laid singly and take around two weeks to hatch

WINGSPAN Up to 4 cm

FLIGHT PERIOD June–August

black eye-spots on both forewings and hind wings

resting butterflies have their wings closed

hairy body

MY OBSERVATIONS

Location: _____

Time/date: _____

The weather is: _____
_____

What have I found? _____
_____

What was it doing? _____
_____
_____
_____

Unlike many butterflies, the beautiful marsh fritillary does not make a camouflaged chrysalis.

MY DRAWINGS AND PHOTOS

I saw this butterfly in: March O   April O   May O   June O

Marsh fritillary _Euphydryas aurinia_

Small populations of these butterflies can be found around the west of the British Isles. Male adults emerge from their pupae before females and set up territories, where they wait for mates. The hairy larvae use silk to fasten the edges of leaves together. They feed inside their 'nests' and benefit from sunny conditions that help them digest food and grow.

ACTUAL SIZE

surface of the wings may be shiny

HABITAT Moors, heaths and damp meadows

BREEDING Hundreds of small yellow eggs are laid in June or July

WINGSPAN 3–5 cm

FLIGHT PERIOD May–July

cream or yellow spots on upperside of wings

SEEN IT?

checked pattern on black background

MY OBSERVATIONS

Location:

Time/date:

The weather is:

What have I found?

What was it doing?

When threatened, these butterflies may flutter their raised wings and flash their eye-spots to scare predators.

♂

MY DRAWINGS AND PHOTOS

I saw this butterfly in: March ○   April ○   May ○   June ○

Meadow brown *Maniola jurtina*

A mong the most common of all British butterflies are meadow browns. Adults feed on nectar from many flowering plants, and the larvae eat grasses. While males often flutter above vegetation looking for mates, females rest near the ground. They usually lay their eggs one at a time and the larvae hatch two to four weeks later.

ACTUAL SIZE

HABITAT Grasslands and gardens

BREEDING Brown larvae hatch from dark eggs, and turn green as they mature

WINGSPAN 4–6 cm

FLIGHT PERIOD June–September

forewings are mostly brown with some orange

males are slightly darker than females

hind wings are brown with a pale fringe

eye-spots

♂

SEEN IT?

MY OBSERVATIONS

Location: _____

Time/date: _____

The weather is: _____

_____

What have I found? _____

_____

What was it doing? _____

_____

_____

_____

MY DRAWINGS AND PHOTOS

The stunning underwings of a painted lady are brightest when young. The colours fade as the butterfly ages.

I saw this butterfly in: March O   April O   May O   June O

Painted lady *Cynthia cardui*

These big butterflies have spectacular, boldly patterned wings. They arrive from North Africa or mainland Europe in spring or summer and visit food plants, sucking up nectar. Their larvae can strip whole plants. They cannot survive the British winter at any stage of their life-cycle, so each summer Britain is recolonized by migrant butterflies.

ACTUAL SIZE

HABITAT Gardens, parks, coasts, farms and wasteland

BREEDING Black, hairy larvae feed on underside of leaves

WINGSPAN 6–7.5 cm

FLIGHT PERIOD March–October

males and females look similar, with black tips and white spots on forewings

long antennae are tipped with white

deep orangey-brown colour

large body

SEEN IT?

MY OBSERVATIONS

Location: _____

Time/date: _____

The weather is: _____

_____

What have I found? _____

_____

What was it doing? _____

_____

_____

_____

In a feeding position, the peacock's bright colours are hidden from view. The dull colours are good camouflage.

MY DRAWINGS AND PHOTOS

I saw this butterfly in: March ○ April ○ May ○ June ○

Peacock _Inachis io_

Often seen on buddleia in summer, peacocks wake from hibernation in spring and mate soon after. Females lay small, green eggs in batches of up to 500, on nettles or hops – the larvae's favourite food. Adults emerge from their pupae from July and feed on nectar from flowers, or on juices from over-ripe fruit. Peacock butterflies live for one year.

ACTUAL SIZE

long antennae used for smelling and touching

HABITAT Flowery gardens and meadows

BREEDING Fully grown larvae are about 4 cm long, and they have black-and-white spots and long, black spines

WINGSPAN 5–7.5 cm

FLIGHT PERIOD March–September

hair on thorax

SEEN IT?

dark brown wing edges

four false eyes on wings

MY OBSERVATIONS

Location: _____

Time/date: _____

The weather is: _____

_____

What have I found? _____

_____

What was it doing? _____

_____

_____

_____

When only the mottled colours and patterns of its underwings are on show, this butterfly blends into its woodland home.

MY DRAWINGS AND PHOTOS

I saw this butterfly in: March ○   April ○   May ○   June ○

Purple emperor *Apatura iris*

Male purple emperors are among the most spectacular of British butterflies, but are rarely seen. They live in broadleaved woodlands in southern England, especially those with oak and willow trees. The blue-green eggs are laid on willow trees and bushes. The larvae are well camouflaged among leaves and they feed on the spring buds.

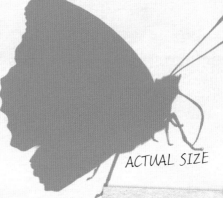

ACTUAL SIZE

HABITAT Woodlands

BREEDING Eggs are laid in trees, and hatch after about ten days

WINGSPAN 7–9 cm

FLIGHT PERIOD June–August

line of white spots

black edges

males have a purple sheen on their wings (females are brown)

eye-spots

long, yellow proboscis

♂

SEEN IT?

MY OBSERVATIONS

Location: _____

Time/date: _____

The weather is: _____

_____

What have I found? _____

_____

What was it doing? _____

_____

_____

_____

The long antennae of a red admiral help it to find the sweet-smelling nectar and rotting fruit it feeds on.

MY DRAWINGS AND PHOTOS

I saw this butterfly in: March ○   April ○   May ○   June ○

Red admiral *Vanessa atalanta*

Primarily a UK migrant, these butterflies are easily recognized by their dark-coloured wings with red bands and white spots. Red admirals are fast, powerful fliers and – unusually for butterflies – may fly at night. These insects are found throughout the UK and Europe in a wide range of habitats.

ACTUAL SIZE

HABITAT Gardens and meadows

BREEDING Single eggs are laid on nettle leaves

WINGSPAN 6 cm

FLIGHT PERIOD March–October

long antennae

red bands on forewings

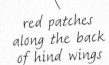

SEEN IT?

red patches along the back of hind wings

edges of wings are lined with blue spots

MY OBSERVATIONS

Location: _____

Time/date: _____

The weather is: _____

_____

What have I found? _____

_____

What was it doing? _____

_____

_____

_____

The ring-like eye-spots that give this butterfly its name are almost invisible when it rests with outspread wings.

MY DRAWINGS AND PHOTOS

I saw this butterfly in: March ○   April ○   May ○   June ○

Ringlet *Aphantopus hyperantus*

ale and female ringlets are almost identical in appearance. They are quite common, and live around Britain in damp or sheltered places. Unlike many other butterflies, ringlets are active in cool, cloudy weather, flying between bramble bushes or thistles to feed. Larvae are cream in colour and hairy.

ACTUAL SIZE

HABITAT Woodlands, hedgerows and damp meadows

BREEDING One generation a year, with adults emerging in June

WINGSPAN 4.5–5 cm

FLIGHT PERIOD June–August

white fringe on the wings

velvety, brown wings

eye-spots

SEEN IT?

MY OBSERVATIONS

Location: _____

Time/date: _____

The weather is: _____

_____

What have I found? _____

_____

What was it doing? _____

_____

_____

_____

These butterflies have an unusual fluttering style of flight, and females often fly in a zigzag pattern.

MY DRAWINGS AND PHOTOS

I saw this butterfly in: March O   April O   May O   June O

Small heath *Coenonympha pamphilus*

Despite their name, these butterflies are not just found on heaths. They are widespread in the British Isles and Ireland, and feed on nectar from a variety of different plants. The small, green larvae are well-hidden from view among grass stems. They usually rest during the day, and feed at night on grass tips. The larvae that hatch near the end of the summer may survive the winter and pupate in April.

ACTUAL SIZE

HABITAT Grasslands, wastelands, sand dunes and heaths

BREEDING Small, green-white eggs are laid one at a time on grass stems

WINGSPAN 3.5 cm

FLIGHT PERIOD May–September

orange patch

eye-spot on underside of forewing

usually rests with wings closed

hind wing underside is brown, cream and grey

SEEN IT?

furry body

MY OBSERVATIONS

Location: _____

Time/date: _____

The weather is: _____

_____

What have I found? _____

_____

What was it doing? _____

_____

_____

_____

Adults may survive the winter by hibernating. The drab colours of the underwings help them to hide in trees and piles of wood.

MY DRAWINGS AND PHOTOS

I saw this butterfly in: March ○   April ○   May ○   June ○

Small tortoiseshell *Aglais urticae*

Common butterflies, small tortoiseshells are often one of the first butterflies to be seen in spring. Adults emerge from hibernation in March or April and mate soon afterwards. They lay their eggs on food plants, such as nettles. The eggs then hatch about ten days later. Small tortoiseshells live in a range of habitats, often around human homes.

ACTUAL SIZE

SEEN IT?

HABITAT Flowery gardens and meadows

BREEDING Heaps of eggs are laid on the underside of nettle leaves in April

WINGSPAN 4–4.5 cm

FLIGHT PERIOD March–September

orange-and-black markings on wings

points on the edges of forewings and hind wings

blue markings along wing edges

MY OBSERVATIONS

Location: _____

Time/date: _____

The weather is: _____

_____

What have I found? _____

_____

What was it doing? _____

_____

_____

_____

Males are often seen resting in sunlit spots, waiting for females. They fight off other males that come too close.

MY DRAWINGS AND PHOTOS

I saw this butterfly in: March ○   April ○   May ○   June ○

Speckled wood Pararge aegeria

These butterflies fly around woodlands and gardens in the summer months. They feed on the sugary substance called honeydew, which is made by aphids. Female speckled woods lay single eggs on grasses, which the larvae feed on when they hatch. The larvae eat and moult for about ten days before turning into chrysalises.

ACTUAL SIZE

HABITAT Woodlands and gardens

BREEDING Larvae are green

WINGSPAN 4 cm

FLIGHT PERIOD March–October

forewings have one black eye-spot

brown, furry body

wings are mottled brown with creamy markings

hind wings have a row of three black eye-spots

SEEN IT?

MY OBSERVATIONS

Location: _____

Time/date: _____

The weather is: _____

_____

What have I found? _____

_____

What was it doing? _____

_____

_____

_____

This wall brown has lost the tip of its forewing. It may have been attacked by a bird while feeding.

MY DRAWINGS AND PHOTOS

I saw this butterfly in: March O   April O   May O   June O

Wall brown *Lasiommata megera*

Often found resting on walls in direct sunlight, wall browns soak up warmth from the sun's rays. Males are more active than females, but look similar. These butterflies are not fussy feeders and take nectar from a range of flowers. Wall browns were once widespread, except in Scotland, but their numbers have dropped dramatically.

ACTUAL SIZE

HABITAT Coastal areas, wastelands and hedgerows

BREEDING Round eggs are often laid on grass, and the larvae are green

WINGSPAN 4.5–5.5 cm

FLIGHT PERIOD May–September

bold orange and brown-black patterns

SEEN IT?

long body with slender abdomen

white-grey fringe

MY OBSERVATIONS

Location: _____

Time/date: _____

The weather is: _____

_____

What have I found? _____

_____

What was it doing? _____

_____

_____

_____

The female has slightly more rounded wings than the male, and its wings are a little deeper in colour.

MY DRAWINGS AND PHOTOS

I saw this butterfly in: March ○   April ○   May ○   June ○

White admiral *Limenitis camilla*

These butterflies have few habitats to choose from because their larvae only feed on honeysuckle plants. White admirals live in woodlands of southern England. Females are slightly bigger than males, but look similar. They lay just one egg at a time on honeysuckle in sheltered places. Adults are strong fliers and glide between trees.

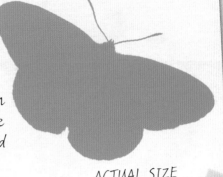

ACTUAL SIZE

antennae tips are orange

HABITAT Woodlands

BREEDING Bright green larvae emerge from small, hairy eggs

WINGSPAN 5.5–6.5 cm

FLIGHT PERIOD June–August

broad, black wings

there may be small patches of red or blue on the wings

white banding across wings

SEEN IT?

MY OBSERVATIONS

Location: _____

Time/date: _____

The weather is: _____
_____

What have I found? _____
_____

What was it doing? _____
_____
_____
_____

When these moths are at rest, their folded wings with mottled colours look like dead or rotting leaves.

MY DRAWINGS AND PHOTOS

I saw this moth in: March ○   April ○   May ○   June ○

Angle shades *Phlogophora meticulosa*

These stunning moths are so well camouflaged that they can be difficult to spot. Adult angle shades are active both day and night, and can be seen throughout the year, although they are more common in summer. Young larvae are often the colour of their food plants, which helps them to avoid predators. Older larvae can rest through the winter.

ACTUAL SIZE

HABITAT Parks, fields, coastal areas and gardens

BREEDING Two generations may be laid in one year, and the larvae are brown or green

WINGSPAN 4–6 cm

FLIGHT PERIOD May–October

slender antennae

furry body

young adults have bands of green, pink or brown on their wings

wings can appear wrinkled, like a dead leaf

SEEN IT?

MY OBSERVATIONS

Location: _____

Time/date: _____

The weather is: _____

_____

What have I found? _____

_____

What was it doing? _____

_____

_____

_____

Unlike many moths, the yellow brimstone holds its wings slightly forward when resting. Females are bigger than males.

MY DRAWINGS AND PHOTOS

I saw this moth in: March ○   April ○   May ○   June ○

Brimstone *Opisthograptis luteolata*

Small, pretty brimstone moths are a distinctive yellow colour. Their wings are marked with small, brown patches, especially along the front edges of the forewings. Brimstones are most active at night, and they fly towards windows and other sources of light. They are most common from spring to autumn. The larvae feast on a range of bushes and other plants.

ACTUAL SIZE

HABITAT Gardens, woodlands, fields and parks

BREEDING Up to three generations a year in southern Britain, but just one in northern places

WINGSPAN 3–4 cm

FLIGHT PERIOD April–October

orange-brown patches on forewings

antennae dip downwards

yellow, rounded body

wings are leaf-shaped

wing colour may be yellow or deep cream

SEEN IT?

MY OBSERVATIONS

Location: _____

Time/date: _____

The weather is: _____

_____

What have I found? _____

_____

What was it doing? _____

_____

_____

_____

The ragwort plant on which the larvae feed is highly poisonous to animals and people.

SEEN IT?

MY DRAWINGS AND PHOTOS

I saw this moth in: March ○   April ○   May ○   June ○

Cinnabar _Tyria jacobaeae_

With their black-and-red wings, cinnabar moths are very distinctive. They rest in low-lying plants during the day and become active at dusk. Cinnabars lay their eggs on ragwort plants in June, and the striped larvae hatch from July onwards. Gold and black stripes on the larvae warn other animals that they taste bad. The larvae form pupae in September and spend winter resting.

ACTUAL SIZE

HABITAT Heaths, wastelands, grassy areas and woodlands

BREEDING Adults produce one generation from May to July, and the larvae feed mostly on ragwort

WINGSPAN 3.5–4 cm

FLIGHT PERIOD May–July

forewings are grey-black with red markings

black body and legs

SEEN IT?

hind wings are red with black borders

MY OBSERVATIONS

Location: _____

Time/date: _____

The weather is: _____

_____

What have I found? _____

_____

What was it doing? _____

_____

_____

_____

The larvae of codling moths eat the fruit of some trees, especially apples and pears.

MY DRAWINGS AND PHOTOS

I saw this moth in: March O   April O   May O   June O

Codling _Cydia pomonella_

The large, eye-shaped markings on the tips of a codling moth's forewings distract and confuse predators, such as birds. Adult females lay a single egg on a leaf of a fruit tree. When the larva emerges, it bores into the fruit, making tunnels as it eats its way through the flesh. The larva pupates under bark or in leaf litter, emerging as an adult between July and October.

ACTUAL SIZE

HABITAT Fruit trees

BREEDING Larvae are also known as apple maggots, and they have white bodies and brown heads

WINGSPAN 1–2 cm

FLIGHT PERIOD July–October

large eyes made up of many small lenses

grey head and body

copper-coloured bands

grey-and-brown mottled wings

SEEN IT?

July O   August O   September O   October O

MY OBSERVATIONS

Location: _____

Time/date: _____

The weather is: _____

_____

What have I found? _____

_____

What was it doing? _____

_____

_____

_____

The stick-like larvae almost disappear when crawling along twigs of their food plants – blackthorn, hawthorn and similar shrubs.

SEEN IT?

MY DRAWINGS AND PHOTOS

I saw this moth in: March ○   April ○   May ○   June ○

Common emerald *Hemithea aestivaria*

The green colour of common emerald moths makes them easy to identify, although the colour fades through the summer. These moths are usually spotted in June and July in southern UK areas, especially around sunset when they emerge from their hiding places. They are rare in northern regions. The larvae feed on a range of shrubs, especially redcurrant, rowan, hawthorn and blackthorn.

ACTUAL SIZE

HABITAT Woodlands, gardens and parks

BREEDING The larvae are green or brown, and stick-like

WINGSPAN 3 cm

FLIGHT PERIOD June–July

long, delicate antennae

white lines may be visible on the wings

SEEN IT?

hind wings have distinctive angles

MY OBSERVATIONS

Location: _____

Time/date: _____

The weather is: _____

_____

What have I found? _____

_____

What was it doing? _____

_____

_____

_____

The larva looks like an elephant's trunk – wide at one end and tapering to the other end. This gives the moth its strange name.

SEEN IT?

MY DRAWINGS AND PHOTOS

I saw this moth in: March ○   April ○   May ○   June ○

Elephant hawk-moth Deilephila elpenor

These beautiful, colourful moths can easily be mistaken for pink butterflies. However, they can be identified as moths by their fat bodies and triangular shape. They are active at night, feeding on nectar from fuchsia, rhododendron and honeysuckle plants. The larvae have large eye-spots on their head-end, but are harmless despite their fearsome appearance.

ACTUAL SIZE

HABITAT Gardens and woodlands

BREEDING The large larvae spend the winter as pupae, hidden in the ground, and the adults emerge in spring

WINGSPAN 7 cm

FLIGHT PERIOD May–July

brightly coloured, plump body

bright pink, olive-green and brown forewings

wings create a characteristic triangle shape

dark patches on hind wings are sometimes visible

SEEN IT?

MY OBSERVATIONS

Location: _____

Time/date: _____

The weather is: _____

_____

What have I found? _____

_____

What was it doing? _____

_____

_____

_____

When this moth spreads its wings out and rests on tree bark, it becomes almost invisible.

MY DRAWINGS AND PHOTOS

I saw this moth in: March ○   April ○   May ○   June ○

Garden carpet *Xanthorhoe fluctuata*

These moths favour gardens and parks where they can find cabbage family plants for their larvae to feed on. The larvae usually only feed at night, so it can be hard to find them. Garden carpet moths may survive the winter, either as larvae or pupae. The larvae build silken cocoons in soil. Adults emerge in April and are active through the summer.

ACTUAL SIZE

HABITAT Gardens, parks and woodlands

BREEDING Several generations from April to October

WINGSPAN 2–3 cm

FLIGHT PERIOD April–September

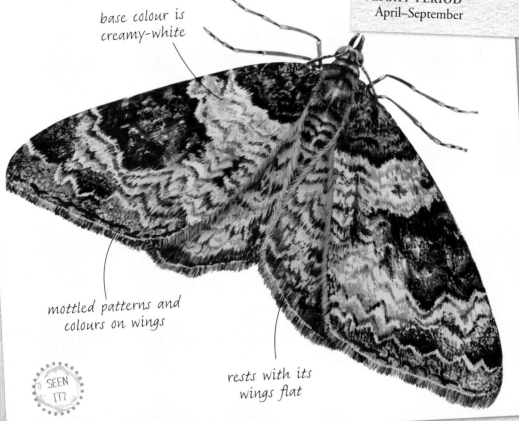

base colour is creamy-white

mottled patterns and colours on wings

SEEN IT?

rests with its wings flat

MY OBSERVATIONS

Location: _____

Time/date: _____

The weather is: _____

_____

What have I found? _____

_____

What was it doing? _____

_____

_____

_____

Garden tiger moths vary in appearance. It is extremely rare to find two adults with identical markings.

MY DRAWINGS AND PHOTOS

I saw this moth in: March ○   April ○   May ○   June ○

Garden tiger *Arctia caja*

With their bold colours, garden tiger moths are easy to spot. The red-coloured hind wings warn other animals to leave them alone, as they taste bad. Garden tigers feed on nectar from flowers. The larvae are brown and black, and are so hairy that they have been named 'woolly bears'. The hairs cause irritation, so they protect the larvae from hungry birds.

ACTUAL SIZE

HABITAT Gardens, farms and open areas

BREEDING Black-and-brown larvae

WINGSPAN 6 cm

FLIGHT PERIOD July–August

long, feathery antennae

fluffy thorax

large forewings are patterned in black-brown and cream

hind wings are red-orange with black-and-blue markings

fat abdomen

SEEN IT?

MY OBSERVATIONS

Location: _____

Time/date: _____

The weather is: _____

_____

What have I found? _____

_____

What was it doing? _____

_____

_____

_____

The moth's curvy forewing edges are described as 'scalloped'. They resemble the curved edges of a scallop shell.

MY DRAWINGS AND PHOTOS

I saw this moth in: March ○   April ○   May ○   June ○

Lime hawk-moth *Mimas tiliae*

These moths can be identified by their wing shape as well as their markings. Lime hawk-moths are common in towns and cities, especially from May onwards. The adults do not feed, but the larvae eat leaves, particularly those of lime trees. Most larvae are green and have yellow stripes. The colours deepen as the larvae age and prepare to pupate.

ACTUAL SIZE

HABITAT Woodlands and gardens

BREEDING Eggs are laid on trees such as lime, elm, birch and elder

WINGSPAN 6–8 cm

FLIGHT PERIOD May–June

olive-green or brown blotches

colours can vary, but the base colour is usually pinkish

wings have a scalloped edge

SEEN IT?

July ○   August ○   September ○   October ○

83

MY OBSERVATIONS

Location: _____

Time/date: _____

The weather is: _____

_____

What have I found? _____

_____

What was it doing? _____

_____

_____

_____

Spiders hate the taste of these colourful larvae, and the adult moths are unaffected by spider venom.

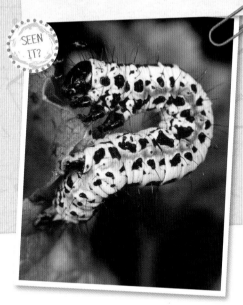

SEEN IT?

MY DRAWINGS AND PHOTOS

I saw this moth in: March ○   April ○   May ○   June ○

Magpie *Abraxas grossulariata*

*B*oldly patterned magpie moths have black-and-white wings with yellow bands. This colouring warns predators, such as birds and spiders, that they taste bad. Adults emerge from their pupae in June and drink nectar from flowers. They can be seen until August and, unlike many other moths, are active during the day.

ACTUAL SIZE

HABITAT Meadows and woods

BREEDING One generation a year, and larvae survive the winter

WINGSPAN 4–5 cm

FLIGHT PERIOD June–August

long antennae

yellow band crosses the forewings

forewings are white with black bands and spots

SEEN IT?

MY OBSERVATIONS

Location: _____

Time/date: _____

The weather is: _____
_____

What have I found? _____
_____

What was it doing? _____
_____
_____
_____

While some poplar hawk-moths have dark, clear patterning, others are paler, with less distinct markings.

MY DRAWINGS AND PHOTOS

I saw this moth in: March O   April O   May O   June O

Poplar hawk-moth *Laothoe populi*

A regular garden visitor, the poplar hawk-moth is one of Britain's largest and most common moths. Adults have a proboscis for feeding, but it is never used. Like many other adult moths, poplar hawk-moths don't feed once they have emerged from the pupa. The larvae are green and have a small tail horn. Older caterpillars have yellow, diagonal stripes on their green bodies. They feed on poplar, aspen and willow trees.

ACTUAL SIZE

HABITAT Woodlands and gardens

BREEDING Usually just one generation a year, but occasionally a second generation emerges in late summer

WINGSPAN Up to 9 cm

FLIGHT PERIOD May–July

a reddish patch on the hind wing is flashed at predators

SEEN IT?

colours may be yellow-brown, reddish, brown or even grey

when at rest, the abdomen curls upwards slightly

hind wing

forewing

MY OBSERVATIONS

Location:

Time/date:

The weather is:

What have I found?

What was it doing?

The large, fleshy larvae have bright green skin, with white and lilac diagonal stripes, and a long 'horn' at the tail end.

SEEN IT?

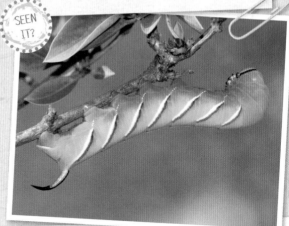

MY DRAWINGS AND PHOTOS

I saw this moth in: March ○   April ○   May ○   June ○

Privet hawk-moth *Sphinx ligustri*

Hawk-moths are usually large and excellent fliers, and privet hawk-moths are no exception. They are common in southern regions of Britain, where they visit gardens in search of privet bushes – the favourite food of their larvae. The moths can be seen resting in the sun during June and July. Male privet hawk-moths make a hissing noise when disturbed to scare predators away.

ACTUAL SIZE

HABITAT Gardens and woodlands

BREEDING Just one generation a year, usually in June or July

WINGSPAN 9–12 cm

FLIGHT PERIOD June–July

slender antennae

striped hind wings are sometimes hidden from view

large body has pink and black bars

SEEN IT?

MY OBSERVATIONS

Location: _____

Time/date: _____

The weather is: _____

_____

What have I found? _____

_____

What was it doing? _____

_____

_____

_____

The moth's upper body, or thorax, is covered in fine hairs. They help to keep flight muscles warm.

MY DRAWINGS AND PHOTOS

I saw this moth in: March ○   April ○   May ○   June ○

Scalloped oak *Crocallis elinguaria*

Living in a wide range of habitats, scalloped oak moths are widespread throughout Britain. Adults emerge from their pupae in summer and fly during July and August. Eggs are laid in summer on broad-leaved trees and bushes, which are the food of the larvae. It is difficult to spot the larvae because they are twig-like and well camouflaged on leafy bushes or trees.

ACTUAL SIZE

HABITAT Gardens, parks, fields and woodlands

BREEDING Eggs survive over the winter and twig-like larvae hatch in spring

WINGSPAN 4–5 cm

FLIGHT PERIOD July–August

SEEN IT?

black spot on forewings

colour can vary from lemon-yellow to brown

hind wings are plain and paler in colour

July ○   August ○   September ○   October ○

MY OBSERVATIONS

Location:

Time/date:

The weather is:

What have I found?

What was it doing?

The larvae have black bodies, with a white or yellow stripe along their backs, as well as rows of spots and stripes.

SEEN IT?

MY DRAWINGS AND PHOTOS

I saw this moth in: March ○   April ○   May ○   June ○

Scarlet tiger *Callimorpha dominula*

These moths live in damp habitats in central and southern regions of England and Wales. The favourite food of their larvae is the comfrey plant, although they also eat brambles and nettles. Scarlet tiger moths are active in the day, feeding on nectar, which they suck from flowers. Their forewings are shiny, which is an unusual feature in moths, but common in butterflies.

ACTUAL SIZE

HABITAT Damp places especially marshes, fens and riverbanks

BREEDING One generation every year, and the larvae are hairy

WINGSPAN 4–6 cm

FLIGHT PERIOD May–June

greenish-black base colour on forewings

rare colours, such as yellow, may be seen

green metallic sheen on the forewings

SEEN IT?

scarlet hind wings

MY OBSERVATIONS

Location:

Time/date:

The weather is:

What have I found?

What was it doing?

Adults live for a short time. Once they have mated, and females have laid their eggs, six-spot burnet moths die.

MY DRAWINGS AND PHOTOS

I saw this moth in: March O   April O   May O   June O

Six-spot burnet *Zygaena filipendulae*

The plump, yellow, black-spotted larvae of six-spot burnet moths feed on bird's-foot trefoil. This wild flower contains a deadly chemical called cyanide, which collects in their bodies. When the larvae become adults, they are still poisonous, and the bright red spots on their wings warn predators to stay away. Six-spot burnet moths are active during the day and feed on nectar. They fly from June to August, and their larvae can survive the winter.

ACTUAL SIZE

HABITAT Meadows, grasslands and coastal areas

BREEDING One generation every year, and the larvae form yellow pupae on grass stems

WINGSPAN 3–4 cm

FLIGHT PERIOD June–August

long antennae

six scarlet spots on each forewing

forewings are black with a bluish sheen

red hind wings with a black fringe

SEEN IT?

About The Wildlife Trusts

Check out The Wildlife Trusts' junior website:

www.wildlifewatch.org.uk

The Wildlife Trusts are committed to conserving local wildlife. There are 47 individual Wildlife Trusts covering every part of the UK, the Isle of Man and Alderney — so there will be one near you, wherever you live.

We have around 2300 nature reserves, looking after all the wildlife habitats found in the UK. They are fantastic places for you and your family to explore and enjoy local wildlife.

Nature reserves can be great places to go to see butterflies and moths. Find reserves near you at www.wildlifetrusts.org/wildlife/reserves.

Wildlife Watch

If you're aged 5–15 and want to find out more about your local wildlife then Wildlife Watch is for you. Members receive a welcome pack, a UK wildlife magazine and poster four times a year — and access to local events and activities! Go to www.wildlifewatch.org.uk/membership for more information.

There are also lots of things to do on the Wildlife Watch website, including spotting sheets to download, games to play and a wildlife diary to keep. You can also keep up to date with wildlife with our monthly e-newsletter, and find out about more than 850 species in the online wildlife database. Just go to www.wildlifewatch.org.uk to register.

See you there!